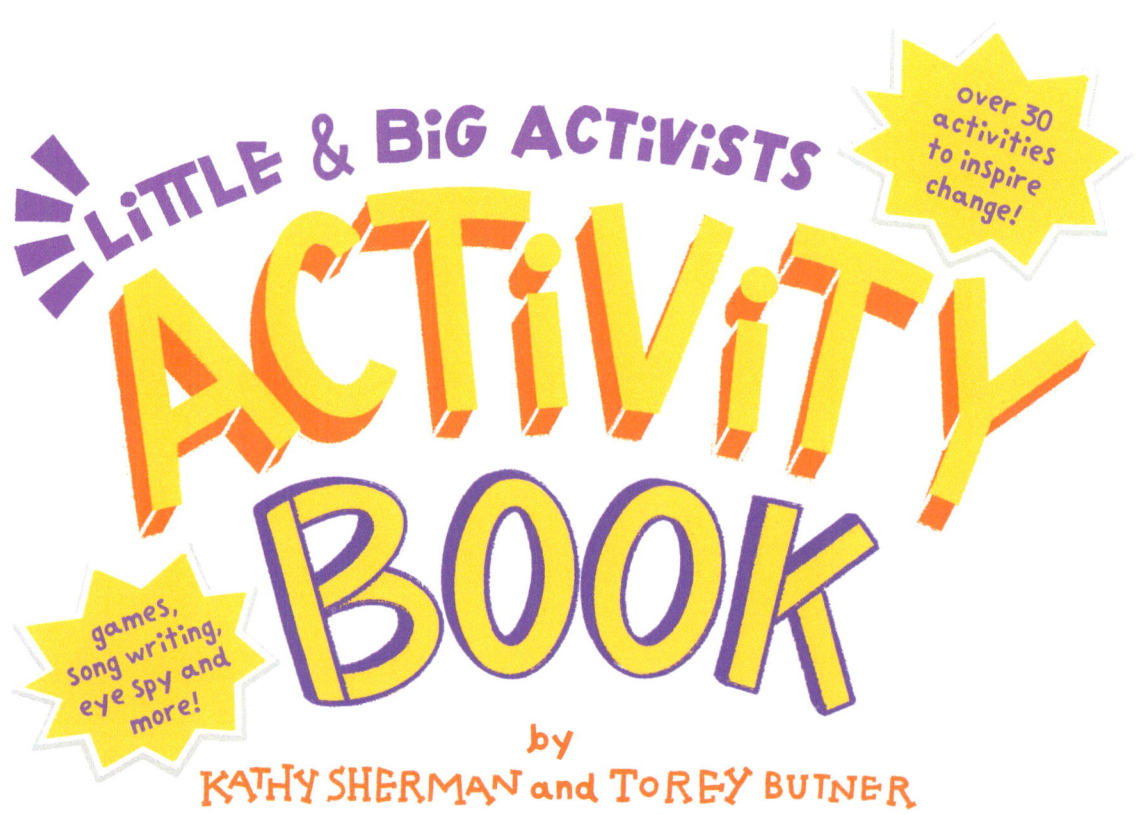

Thank you to all of the teachers, parents and children who give me hope, every day, that we can make this a wonderful world. A very special shout out to Torey Butner whose artwork is beyond amazing. Thank you to my own children, my beautiful boys who are now beautiful men and to my own wonderful husband. This book is dedicated to all of you!

• Kathy Sherman •

For my amazing family and friends that help me keep moving forward.

• Torey Butner •

©2023 Kathy Sherman and Torey Butner

All rights reserved. No portion of this book may be reproduced - mechanically, electronically, or by any other means with the exception of photocopying for teaching purposes in classrooms - without written permission of Kathy Sherman.

Library of Congress Cataloging-in-Publication Data is available.

ISBN 979-8-9888381-3-5

printed in the USA
First printing August 2023

goodfolksongs.com

LITTLE & BIG ACTIVISTS ACTIVITY BOOK

over 30 activities to inspire change!

games, song writing, eye spy and more!

by
KATHY SHERMAN and TOREY BUTNER
illustrated by TOREY BUTNER

from the award-winning album
LET'S SING! SONGS FOR LITTLE ACTIVISTS/SONGS FOR BIG ACTIVISTS

LITTLE OR BIG ACTIVIST...

You can make a world of a difference.

(your name)

Draw a picture of yourself here!

READ ME!
(You'll be glad you did!)

This activity book is meant to be a companion piece to the album,

Let's Sing! Songs for Little Activists/ Let's Sing! Songs for Big Activists

If you don't have the album, **DO NOT DELAY**, go get it right now! We'll wait... Go on... go... now...

(You can find it on many streaming platforms, there is really no excuse!)

Turning art into activism!

Each song on the album deals with a specific topic that is worth further exploration **as a family OR in a classroom.**

Topics such as...

community building

climate change

peace

recycling & kindness

for the younger children,

gun violence   **communication (or lack of it)**   **war**

& drought for the older folks.

(I know this might sound fairly grim but these are important topics to explore if we're going to make a difference in the world, right?)

There are several pages of activities dedicated to each song. The Songs for Little Activists have activities that are appropriate for K-3.

The Songs for Big Activists include discussion topics, ideas for volunteer activities, letter writing campaigns, protest marches and social media ideas.

Find Your Style!

Being out in the front line of a march or a movement is not for everyone. Some of us are more comfortable playing quieter, more subtle roles in being activists. It's oK.

Just by being kind you are making a huge difference in someone's life.

7

Contents

Every song is a call to action. Sometimes that call is a tiny seed planted deep into your heart, sometimes it's a siren blaring into your ear. Most of the time a song's message lies somewhere in between. Each activity we present will give you and your children an opportunity to think, discover, and discuss the healing of the world.

Songs for Little Activists

These activities will delight children from pre K-3rd grade. Some are art projects, others are ideas for family activities and discussions.

1. Sing for the Climate
•Working Together•
An anthem for the whole CD. If we work together we can get something really important done.
Page 10

2. Song of Peace
•Community & Peace•
The value of being a community, gathering friends and family to achieve a dream.
Page 18

3. If I Had a Hammer
•Speak Up•
"If you can say it, you can sing it!" Empowering kids to use their words.
Page 22

4. Recycle Round
•Recycle & Reuse•
Activities to help teach recycling and reusing materials around us.
Page 28

5. Teaching Peace
•Setting an Example•
When children model acts of peace it can be a powerful experience for grown-ups. We can learn a lot from children!
Page 36

6. IT COULD BE A WONDERFUL WORLD

•Warmth, Compassion, Kindness•
These are the ingredients for a wonderful world.
Page 40

7. SOMOS EL BARCO

•Connection & Community•
We are all in the same "boat". Each of us are connected by our humanity.
Page 44

Songs for Big Activists

These activities are geared toward older children, teens and adults. They include ideas that require a bit more effort, thoughtful discussion and action.

8. THE TIMES THEY ARE A CHANGIN'

•Change•
Change is inevitable. Learn to make thoughtful decisions to change the world for the better.
Page 52

9. ONE FOOT IN FRONT OF THE OTHER / LEAD WITH LOVE

•Leading•
It's scary being a leader but sometimes you have to be THAT person.
Page 58

10. CLEAN, SAFE, WATER

•Water Conservation•
Water is life! We must be careful to protect our most precious reource.
Page 62

11. SINGING FOR OUR LIVES

•Standing Up•
This song teaches us why we need to stand up together against gun violence.
Page 66

12. WHERE HAVE ALL THE FLOWERS GONE?

•Anti-War•
This anthem gently reminds us about the futility of war.
Page 70

Sing for the Climate

Lyrics by Nic Balthazar, Stef Kamil Carlens, Music is a traditional Italian song "Bella Ciao"

Performed on the Let's Sing! Songs for Little Activists/ Songs for Big Activists album in the key of Bm then goes to Cm

Help build your community. Draw yourself taking action!

Singing for the Climate

This song was the soundtrack for a video petition to encourage the Belgium Prime Minister, the State Secretary of Environment and the Flemish and European Ministers of Environment to sign on to the demands of the "Campaign for the Climate".

I urge all you out there to use this recording to make your own statements for climate actions **NOW!**

Community Building

Building a better future starts with our community! Think about what you enjoy doing already. Is there a way to bring that to your community? (e.g. if you enjoy baking, can you hold a bake sale and donate the money to a cause you care about?)

Write down your ideas on the next page!

Building your Community Brainstorm

1. Organize a toy swap

2. Volunteer at the pet shelter

3.

4.

5.

6.

7.

8.

9.

10.

11.

12.

Make the world greener

Draw your imaginary garden! Think about what you want to include. Are there vegetables? What insects and animals do you see?

Make the world cleaner

How can you clean inside and outside your living environment? See how many of these you can check off your list!

- ☑ Make food from leftovers
- ☐ Turn off the lights
- ☐ Throw away your trash
- ☐ Turn off the water when you brush your teeth
- ☐ _____ (fill in your own!)

- ☑ Use cold water
- ☐ Pick up your clothes
- ☐ Recycle cans, bottles, paper, books and toys
- ☐ Unplug your chargers when you're not using them
- ☐ _____ (fill in your own!)

15

Write your own song about what you want to change

Speak up about something you feel isn't right through song!

First! Think about a few things that you want to change. Do you want longer recess time? Maybe a better playground? Or even climate change?

_____

_____

What do we need to do to make these changes?

_____

_____

_____

Title: _____

~~~~~~~~~~

We need to _____
_____,

We need to _____
_____,

We need to open our eyes and do it now, now, now

We need to build _____
_____,

And we **need to start right now!**

SONG OF PEACE

by Lorre Wyatt

Performed on the Let's Sing! Songs for Little Activists/Songs for Big Activists album in the key of D

What do you want to be when you grow up?

Draw two jobs you want when you grow up!

Dreaming Big

This song offers the idea that nothing is impossible if we work hard and we work together.

Draw your favorite activities and objects.
Think about: what do you want to be when you grow up?

Don't forget to dream as big as you can!
Nothing is out of reach!

Corn Maze

Start at one end and find your way to the other end!

Start   End

IF I HAD A HAMMER

by Pete Seeger and Lee Hayes
Performed on the Let's Sing! Songs for Little Activists/ Songs for Big Activists album in the key of G

Written in 1949 as an anthem for many **progressive** (This means believing in changes!) concerns of the day, "The Hammer Song" still feels relevant today.

Take a moment to think about how this song can apply today!

We have many **TOOLS** for change at our disposal. Let's use them! Let's raise our **VOICES** when we see injustices done. Let's **WORK** to keep our planet healthy. Let's **SING** to stay joyful!

Hammer Mad Libs

Use the word bank below to fill in the blanks to complete the song!

If I had a _____,
(noun)

I'd _____ it in the _____,
(verb) (time of day)

I'd _____ it in the _____,
(verb) (time of day)

all over this _____.
(location)

Word Bank:

ring   bell   evening
hammer   morning   land

Your Mad Libs

Make your very own mad libs song! Fill out the word bank with words you come up with yourself. Let your imagination soar!

Word Bank:

Nouns: _____

_____

Verbs: _____

_____

Times of day: _____

_____

Location: _____

_____

If I had a _____ ,

(noun)

I'd _____ it in the _____ ,

(verb) (time of day)

I'd _____ it in the _____ ,

(verb) (time of day)

all over this _____ .

(location)

25

What Will Your Sign Say?

Words hold power and when put on a sign, you can share your thoughts and beliefs! Write a few signs here!

RECYCLE

One metal can,
two metal cans,
Three metal cans,
A

Don't throw your trash in my backyard
My backyard, my backyard
Not in the forest
The river or the stream

Cardboard boxes
Racecars, guitars
Castles, spaceships
Fly me to the moon.

Tin Bird Feeder

Cans are a great opportunity to show how you can recycle! Follow these steps to make your own bird feeder out of a can! Ask your grownup to help you find a child safe can.

1 Collect your materials: can, masking tape, string, bird seeds.

2 Add masking tape around the rim. Tie the string around the can.

3 Fill the can with bird seeds.

4 Find a place to hang your bird feeder to feed the birds!

Cardboard Kazoos

Make a kazoo out of a cardboard toilet tube following these steps!

1 Collect your materials: cardboard toilet tube, scissors, tape, pen and parchment paper.

2 Cut the rolls in half. Now you can make two kazoos and share!

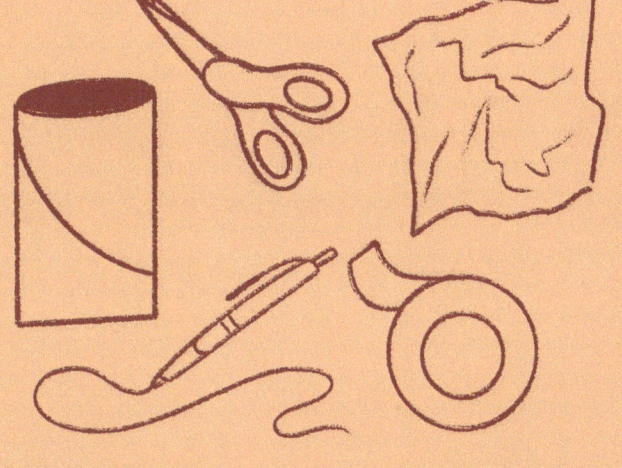

3 Make a small air hole in the tube for a better tone.

4 Experiment with the tightness of the parchment paper.

 Bring this into real life! Play along to the songs with your new kazoo!

Cardboard Structures in the World

There are many ways people use cardboard around the world, building structures is one of them!

Cardboard bicycle by Phil Bridges

Christchurch cardboard cathedral, photo by Tony Hisgett

Church in New Zealand made with cardboard tubes.

32

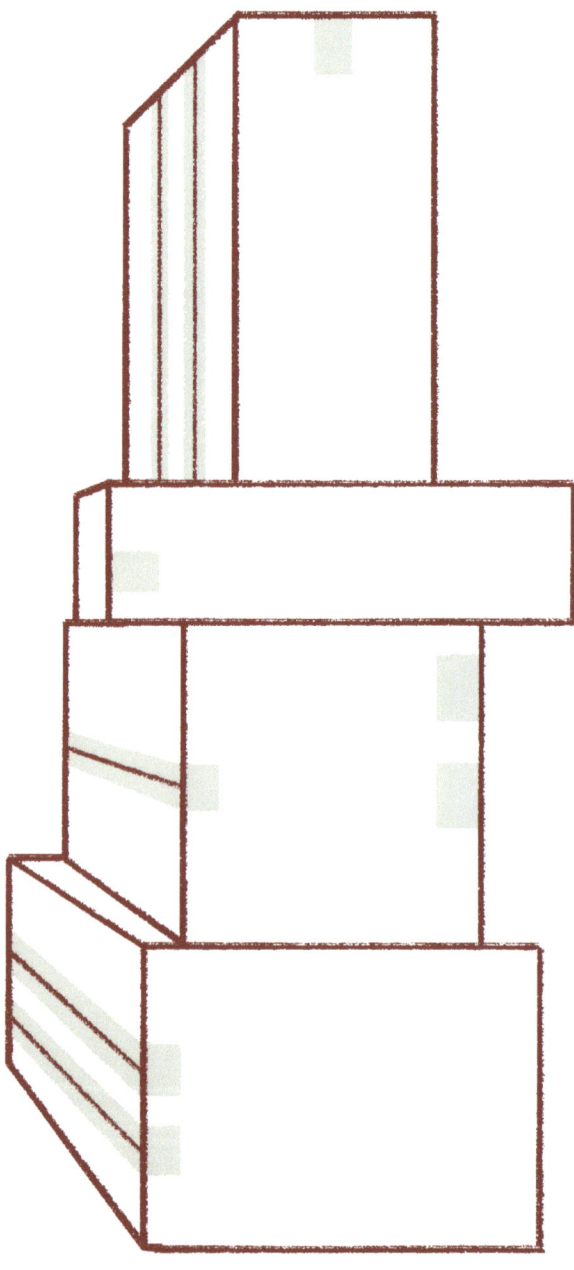

Use these cardboard boxes for your creation!

Cardboard Creation

What would your cardboard creation be?
- Castle?
- Space ship?
- Fort?
- Boat?
- Race car?
- _____?

Food Waste

Did you know that FOOD WASTE is one of the BIGGEST contributors to climate change??

When food goes into the landfill and rots, it produces methane, a greenhouse gas that is even more dangerous and potent than carbon dioxide.

When we waste food, we also waste the energy and water it takes to grow, harvest, transport and package it.

For more good ideas and recipes, check the:

United Nations Climate Action Website

https://www.un.org/en/climatechange/science/climate-issues/food

Let's EAT SMARTER

- Try to eat a more plant based diet.

- Eat food that is local (if possible).

- Think about how much you prepare.

- Eat your leftovers!

- If you need to throw out your food, compost your rotting fruits and vegetables.

- Bring your reusable shopping bags.

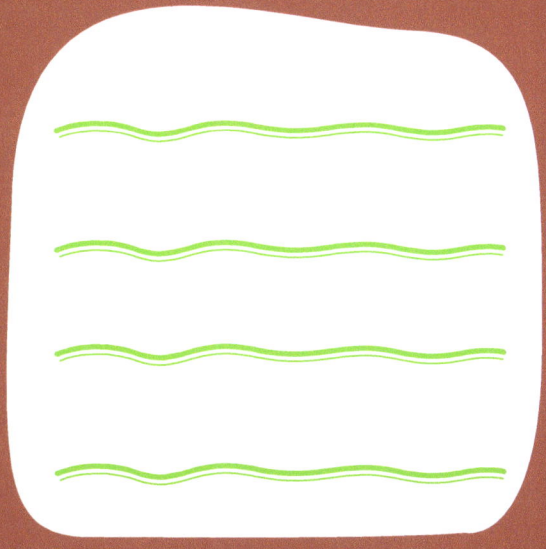

(fill in your own!)

Compost 👁 Spy

Find the items that belong in the compost bin!

35

by Red Grammer, performed on the Let's Sing! Songs for Little Activists/Songs for Big Activists album in the key of Bb

Whenever I sing this song I imagine a whole group of children marching in a parade — a Peace Brigade — singing that they will be teaching the grown-ups of the world how to behave respectfully to one another, how to engage in civilized discourse when we disagree, and how to be a kind and generous friend.

Teaching Peace

You have the best smile!

Your inside is just as beautiful as your outside.

I am really glad we met.

You make me float like I'm on millions of bubbles!

I know that if you ever make a mistake, you fix it.

Nothing can stop you!

IT COULD BE A WONDERFUL WORLD

**Lyrics by Hy Zaret, Music by Lou Singer
Slightly updated lyrics by Kathy Sherman
Performed on the Let's Sing! Songs for Little Activists/
Songs for Big Activists album in the key of G**

Here is another timeless song. In 1947, the songwriters were commissioned by a radio station to write a series of songs on "racial understanding and Americanism." What they wrote became the album "Little Songs on Big Subjects". It has since been re-released as "It Could Be a Wonderful World".

Note: Some lyrics in the songs have been changed to be more gender inclusive.

Color in your wonderful world!

What would the signs say?

What would the world look like if everyone were kind to each other?

What would you see in the window?

DRAW YOUR NEIGHBORHOOD

What would your neighborhood look like if everyone were kind to each other? How would people act? What would the houses look like?

THE STICKY NOTE WALL!

Even just a simple hello can make someone's day. Write kind things on these sticky notes!

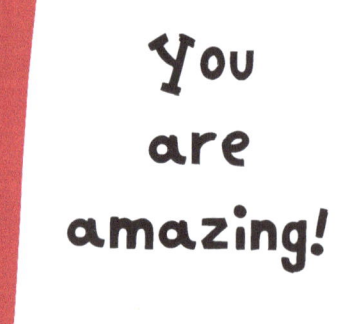

SOMOS EL BARCO

by Lore Wyatt, performed on the Let's Sing! Songs for Little Activists/Songs for Big Activists album in the key of A

The stream sings it to the river,
The river sings it to the sea.

Same Boat

We share the world with people and animals alike! Draw the animals and people who are all in the same boat as we are!

A Letter to a Friend

Write a sweet letter to a friend using the prompts below.

Dear _____

I like how _____ you are.

I think you're amazing at _____
_____

_____

And it's always fun when we
_____

_____

together. Thanks for being my friend!

From,

_____

Family Kindness Jar

Write kind notes to your family below! Bring it into real life: Make a family kindness jar that you can drop notes into and read with your family.

I love how much my family cares about each other

Community Kindness Jar

Write kind notes to your community below! You can write notes to friends, babysitters, teachers, custodians, mail carriers, supermarket clerks or someone else in your community.

My friend is the best!

A Letter to a Grownup

Write a sweet letter to a grownup using the prompts below.

Dear _____

You are _____
           (kind word here.)

It always makes me smile when we

_____

_____
_____ together.
(something fun that you do with your grownup.)

You are more amazing than

_____
           (something amazing.)

Thanks for being my _____

From,

_____

The Times They Are A Changin'

Even though it was written 60 years ago, the times really haven't changed at all! We seem to be fighting the same battles we fought 60 years ago. We still are at war, we still have corrupt politicians, we still have parents and children who can't understand each other. The more times change, the more they stay the same. Perhaps the real genius of this song is that it is a song for all times.

Dear _____,
(legislator name)

I am a _____.
(are you a student?)

I am writing to _____
(reason why you are writing)

_____

_____

_____

Sincerely,

_____
(your name here)

_____
(legislator's full name)

_____
(address)

_____

SEND MAIL

Writing letters to your legislator (person who makes the laws) is a great way to make a difference!
Get your grownup to help you.

Here are things to think about when writing your letter:
- What topic do you want to pick?
- What have you learned about the topic that you can talk about?
- Why do you want something to change?

- Cut out your postcard and write your note.
- Make sure you address it properly. Follow the directions on the previous page and ask your grownup for help.

2.
- Buy a stamp.
- A stamp is proof of payment for your postcard. If you don't have a stamp, the post office can't send it. You can usually buy stamps directly from the post office.
- Apply the stamp in the box on the previous page.

- Mail your postcard.
- Find a post office or a public mail box to drop in your note.

Get Involved!

One of the very best organizations that helps curate the many different civil liberties and civil rights issues we as a country are facing today is the ACLU. Their "grassroots army" is called People Power:

- https://www.peoplepower.org

Here you will find all sorts of opportunities for letter writing, phone calls, demonstrations, organizing, strategizing. It's a wonderful resource.

Create an Oral History

Interview your grandparents, parents, aunts, uncles, neighbors...(This should be someone you like). Find out about their lives. Come with a list of prepared questions. Simple questions can lead to some very interesting answers. Be prepared to be surprised. Your elders are probably way cooler than you can imagine!

ADDED BONUS: Having a sound and/or video recording of them telling their stories is something you can cherish.

Prompt List of Questions

1. What was life like when you were a child?

2. Did you have a pet?

3. Where were you born?

4. Did you like school?

5.

6.

7.

One Foot in Front of the Other

by Melanie DeMore
performed on the Let's Sing! Songs for Little Activists/
Songs for Big Activists album in the key of Am

Melanie DeMore is an inspiring songwriter, composer, activist, teacher, singer, human. I can't even really capture all the nouns, verbs and adjectives to describe this superstar. All I can say is that if you need some inspiration to get you through your day, check her out.

This song is about offering love and support to those around you. Sometimes you are going to be the one tapped on the shoulder to be the leader. It's scary but YOU can do it. You just need to put one foot in front of the other and lead with love. There will be lots of people around you to help and give you all the support and encouragement you need.

A wonderful family activity that supports the spirit of this song is donating to organizations helping people who are disadvantaged:

- Organizing food and clothing drives,
- Donating to local food banks
- Family Giving Tree. This is a group that gathers holiday wishes from disadvantaged children and then collects donated gifts, wraps them, and delivers them to these children. (https://familygivingtree.org)

Make a Plan

Sometimes, all you need to lead with confidence and courage is to make a plan.

Focus on one of your goals. What are the steps you need to take to get to your goal? Fill this out with your grownup.

_____   _____

_____   _____

_____   _____

_____

Now that you've filled out all the steps, go through and number each step to make your plan!

Clean, Safe, Water

Music: Bob Nolan
Lyrics: Kathy and Len Sherman

```
G                     D
Each day we run, and have our fun
G              D           G
We drink and play in water, cool water
        C                D
Some children sigh, with their throats
so dry
         G          C     G    D
They wait in line for water, clear, clean,
G
water
```

The fishes roam in their ocean home
And the coral sway in water, clear, water
Our gardens grow from the seeds we sow
Their thirsty roots need water, cool, clean water

```
Chorus
G                         D
Listen to the land it's telling you to stand
         G                D
Every woman, every man save all you can
    G
of water
    C
The birds and the bees
    G
The critters in the seas
    C                   D
And all of the people in the world agree
               G     C
Save our water, ooh
G       D    G
Clean, safe, water
```

The plastic in the sea
and the oil on the beach
There's a lesson we must teach about water
Precious water

When there's nowhere left to go if the water doesn't flow
We need to take it slow and be careful how we
Use our water,
our precious water

Chorus
Listen to the land it's telling you to stand
Every woman, every man save all you can
of water

The birds and the bees
The critters in the seas
And all of the people in the world agree
Save our water, ooh
Clean, safe, water
Cool, clear, water

Clean, Safe Water

Lyrics by Kathy and Len Sherman, Music by Bob Nolan

Many of you will recognize this song as the old Sons of the Pioneers song "Cool, Clear Water". I felt this was the perfect song for updating (with permission from the publisher) to reflect on the water crisis that we now are experiencing due to climate change. Some parts of the world are experiencing catastrophic flooding while others are experiencing terrifying wildfires due to drought conditions. The oceans are polluted with enough plastic to form a continent and shore birds are being poisoned by oil spills. Populations around the world are suffering from the lack of clean drinking water and therefore there is an increase in water-borne diseases. It's not a pretty picture. — Save our water, our precious water.

Plastic Clean Up

All these products have plastic.
"X" out the items that don't belong in the ocean!

Clean local beaches

We can clean our local beaches and keep our ocean safe! Here are the materials you will need to clean your local beach!

- ☐ Trash bags
- ☐ First aid kit
- ☐ Hand sanitizer
- ☐ Wipes
- ☐ Large coolers of water
- ☐ Work gloves
- ☐ Waterbottles
- ☐ Sunscreen
- ☐ Bug Spray

Want to do more?

Check out these organizations:

- Natural Resources Defense Council (NRDC) is great at the federal level.
- https://www.nrdc.org

- Acterra organizes local creek cleanups, and so much more for renewable energy, education, workshops and more. While they are local to the Bay Area, much of what they do is online and can be accessed across the country.
- https://www.acterra.org

Singing For Our Lives

by Holly Near
originally performed by the SF Gay Men's Chorus
to commemorate Harvey Milk and Mayor George Moscone
Performed on the Let's Sing! Songs for Little Activists/
Songs for Big Activists album in the key of C

```
C              F              C
We are a gentle, angry people
              G                          C G C
And we are Singing, Singing for our lives x2
```

We are a land of many colors
And we are Singing, Singing for our lives x2

We are young and old together
And we are Singing, Singing for our lives x2

We are queer and straight together*
And we are Singing, Singing for our lives x2

We are trans and cis together
And we are Singing, Singing for our lives x2

We are a justice seeking people
And we are Singing, Singing for our lives x2

We are a gentle, loving people
And we are Singing, Singing for our lives x2

*This verse honors our trans community and is not in the original song.

Singing for our Lives
by Holly Near

> "We are gentle, angry people, and we are singing for our lives!"

This really sums up what this album is about. Holly Near wrote this song after San Francisco Supervisor Harvey Milk and Mayor George Moscone were gunned down in 1978.

It has become an anthem of unity for all people, whatever color, creed, gender identity or age.

It is sung all over the world.

We are Singing for our Lives!

Resources

Here are some well-vetted organizations committed to ending gun violence:

• Amnesty International (ending gun violence)
https://www.amnesty.org/en/what-we-do/arms-control/gun-violence/

• Sandy Hook Promise (started by parents who lost a child during mass shooting at Sandy Hook) Elementary School
https://www.sandyhookpromise.org

• Brady Campaign (started by former press secretary to President Reagan who was paralyzed by gun violence)
https://www.bradyunited.org

• Giffords Center for Violence Intervention (started by former AZ congresswoman who nearly lost her life to gun violence)
https://giffords.org

Where have all the flowers gone?

GRAVEYARDS

SOLDIERS

Where Have all the Flowers Gone?

Here are the chords that I play on this recording. With a bit of ingenuity you can figure out where they go.

> **Key of F: Capo 3 and play these chords:**
> D Bm G A
> D Bm G A
> D Bm G A
> G D G A D

I and many other artists have condensed the verses "girls --> husbands, men --> soldiers." Instead we sing "children --> soldiers."

I feel this actually has a greater impact especially as there are still many child soldiers out there, not to mention our own, young men and women who sign up for active military duty, possibly to experience the glory of war,

> **when they don't really understand how precious a human life is.**

72

Activies & Discussion Questions

We can learn from artists about the high price of war:

- ☐ Visit war memorials
- ☐ Check out museums
- ☐ Seek out exhibits dealing with the aftermath of war. There are often exhibits by refugee children.

NOTE: Some museum exhibits have very stark images of war devastation that might not be suitable for the youngest of children.

When visiting museums and war memorials with young children, sometimes it is best to wait for them to ask questions rather than forcing any issues.

- Why is there war?
- What is happening to the people there?
- Is there such a thing as a "Good War"?
- When is war justified?
- Can we help?

Cherishing our Children

Every culture, every country has experienced war at some point in history. Somewhere in our collective DNA we carry the sorrow and loss created by war. It is up to us as parents and educators to teach our children that

> war is ugly, not glorious.
> It is painful and destructive.

> "Every war is a war against the child."
> – Eglantyn Jebb, 1876-1928,
> founder of Save the Children.

Jebb drafted the Declaration of the Rights of the Child 1924, also known as the Geneva Declaration, "recognizing that mankind owes to the Child the best that it has to give, declare and accept it as their duty that, beyond and above all considerations of race, nationality or creed."

> Write a letter on the next page to a loved one to make sure they know that you love them.

date _____

Dear _____
(who are you writing to?)

I just wanted to tell you I like how

_____ you are.

You're amazing at _____.

We always have fun together when we

_____

_____

_____.

From,

_____
(your name here)

Alternatives to Military Service

Practically every country has compulsory civil service when young people graduate from high school.

The mandatory draft in the US ended in 1973, however all young male US citizens must register for the draft when they turn 18 years old.

Currently we have an all volunteer army but that can change if the US goes to war.

Some might feel the call to enlist.

Others might feel the call to serve their country in other ways.

Resources

Regardless of the state of the world, here are some alternatives to joining the armed forces:

- Seeking higher education at a four year college or university

- Attending a vocational college or community college

- Serving in AmeriCorps (www.americorps.gov)

- Serving in the Peace Corps (www.peacecorcorps.gov)

- Consider volunteering for a non-government agency (Habitat for Humanity, City Year, Red Cross, Meals on Wheels)

Write or Draw Your Own Comic

Especially interesting for tweens and teens is the history of Manga and Anime, much of which emerged from the devastation of World War II.

Hayao Miyazaki, the great Japanese storyteller, animator, director, screenwriter, manga artist and co-founder of Studio Ghibli poignantly explores the grief caused by war in his movies Grave of the Fireflies, Porco Rosso, Princess Mononoke, Castle in the Sky, Nausica of the Valley of the Wind and others.

Title:

Setting:

Characters:

Problem:

What happens next?

How is the problem fixed?

www.ingramcontent.com/pod-product-compliance
Lightning Source LLC
Chambersburg PA
CBHW041423010526
44119CB00015B/354